SUPERTEAM UNITED

The Stars making Old Trafford History

UNOFFICIAL
GUIDE

CONTENTS

Magpie Books Ltd
7 Kensington Church Court
London W8 4SP

ISBN 0-75251-836-4

ALEX FERGUSON	4
PAUL SCHOLES	5
STEVE BRUCE	6
MANCHESTER UNITED FC HISTORY	8
ERIC CANTONA	10
PETER SCHMEICHEL	12
GARY PALLISTER	14
NICKY BUTT	15
STORY OF A SEASON	16
DENIS IRWIN	20
GARY NEVILLE	21
RYAN GIGGS	22
LEE SHARPE	24
THE SUPERTEAM CHALLENGE	26
ANDY COLE	28
ROY KEANE	30
THE SUPERTEAM CHALLENGE – ANSWERS	32

This independent publication has been prepared without any involvement on the part of Manchester United Football Club or the Premier League.

More has been written about Manchester United than any other football club in the world. Wherever you may roam, the name is guaranteed to bring smiles and nods of recognition...not to mention the names of 'Bob-bee Chairl-ton' and 'Den-eez Lore'. Just ask Dennis Bergkamp, whose dad named him after the 1960s' goal ace – even if he did add an extra 'n'!

But more and more these days, the names you'll hear are Giggs, Cole and Cantona – today's legends, and men who've brought success to Old Trafford that equals anything in United's proud history. The first ever two Premier League Championships found their way to Manchester, and though Blackburn managed to wrest the trophy across Lancashire, United were giving it all they'd got in '96 to make it three out of four...not to mention a Cup Final showdown with Liverpool.

It all added up to 'house full' notices and a waiting list for season tickets as long as the East Lancs Road, as supporters from all corners of the country clamoured to get in to the newly redeveloped Old Trafford. Truth is, though, you'd have to play at a Wembley-sized stadium week in week out to seat even half of the people who want to witness legends in the making.

When the history of football is written, expect the name of Manchester United to feature first and foremost. That's the way it's always been – and you'd best believe the players featured here aim to keep it that way!

FERGUSON

When he first arrived at Old Trafford in late 1986, Alex Ferguson CBE had a hard act to follow – not just Big Ron Atkinson, the last man in the hot seat, but Sir Matt Busby, that legend among managers, whose reputation had overshadowed each and everyone who'd followed him.

Alex, the Glasgow-born son of a shipyard worker, believed he had the ability to build his own team – one that could rival the glorious names of Charlton, Law and Best and before that the Busby Babes whose dreams of glory were shattered at Munich.

Fergie's quest reached fruition when he led his United to their first title in 26 years. It was the first ever Premier League season – and the second saw the Red Devils on top again. And though Blackburn denied the Old Trafford team an historic treble, it was business as usual again in 1995-96 as the side, led by Steve Bruce and fuelled by the flair of Scholes, Giggs and Cantona, won through to the Cup Final as well as turning the Premiership into a two-horse race and snatching the lead after being 12 points behind.

Yet the Scot with the steely exterior showed precious few signs of emotion. He'd been there, done that, written the book...yet the will to win still burned just as fiercely within as it had when he played in the Scottish League for teams as large as Rangers and as small as Queens Park, his first port of call in 1957.

Managerial honours have come thick and fast – the FA Cup (1990 and 1994), Cup Winners' Cup and European Super Cup (1991), League Cup (1992) and the first two Premier Leagues. This past, glorious season, is just the icing on the cake.

Did You Know?

Alex briefly managed Scotland after the death of the late great Jock Stein but declined to make it permanent.

ALEX FERGUSON *Managerial Record*

FROM	TO	CLUB
July 1974	October 1974	East Stirling (player-manager)
October 1974	April 1978	St Mirren
June 1978	November 1986	Aberdeen
November 1986		Manchester United

SCHOLES

Paul 'Supersub' Scholes is the latest and some would say greatest of Alex Ferguson's Brilliant Bairns that look set to give Busby's Babes a rival in the history books. Yet while the Nevilles ply their trade at the back and Butt and Beckham bolster the midfield, it's up front where it hurts that Scholesey flourishes. A wisdom far beyond his 21 years seems to inhabit that distinctive red head – and talking of heading, he doesn't half get some height for a wee fella of just five foot six.

The past season has seen Premier League defences fighting to get to grip with Scholes the scoring sensation. He started off in the first team, but for many games was taken out of the action prior to the final whistle. He then took up residence on the bench himself...and one man to feel his hot breath on his collar has been Andy Cole, who more than once has ended the match on the bench as Supersub took his bow. And in the ultimate compliment, Eire manager Mick McCarthy has discovered an Irish grandparent that gives England youth cap Paul two international routes to choose from.

In almost any other club, Paul Scholes would be a first-team regular by now. Hopefully he won't follow the likes of Mark Robins out of Old Trafford – but one has the feeling Alex Ferguson wouldn't risk it!

PAUL SCHOLES *Factfile*

Born:	16 November 1974
Birthplace:	Salford
Height:	5' 6"
Weight:	10st 8lb

League Record (To start of 1995-96 season)

FROM-TO	CLUB	APPS	GOALS
1994-95	Manchester United	17	5

“You could see the ability he had from the beginning. We all knew he could go far in the game. Sometimes you can see the fear in young players when they take the field at United with 40,000 people there. There was no fear in Paul – you could tell it was what he wanted. **”**

MARK HUGHES

BRUCE

The arrival of million-pound David May from Blackburn at the start of the 1994-95 season, suggested that Manchester United might soon be saying goodbye to its captain courageous, Steve Bruce.

That's where the story diverted from reality, though. The old warhorse refused to give up his position gracefully, continuing to exert his powerful influence from the back while moving forward to snatch important goals at corners and free-kicks, thanks to his power in the air and shrewd timing of runs.

It remains a disappointment that a single England B cap is as near as the likeable Geordie is going to get to international recognition. 'I'm a great believer that what you never had you never miss,' he says. Besides, since Newcastle, Sunderland and Sheffield Wednesday all rejected him after trials, this late developer is happy to be playing professional football at all!

He's been a regular choice at every one of his three League clubs ever since signing pro at Gillingham in 1978. Steve played over 200 League games for the Kent side before putting a cool £125,000 into their coffers in 1984 by moving on to Norwich. Three and a half seasons at Carrow Road saw him mature into one of the League's most promising defenders.

It was no surprise, then, to soccer watchers when United made their £800,000 move just before Christmas 1987. And what a present he turned out to be! An ever-present in his first full season, he's since picked up every honour domestic football has to offer, as well as playing a major part in the European Cup Winners' Cup success of 1991.

STEVE BRUCE *Factfile*

Born:	31 December 1960
Birthplace:	Corbridge
Height:	6'
Weight:	12st 6lb

League Record (To start of 1995-96 season)

FROM-TO	CLUB	APPS	GOALS
1979-84	Gillingham	205	29
1984-87	Norwich City	141	14
1987-95	Manchester United	279	35
Total		625	78

" It was the biggest thrill of my life to find that United wanted me. I needed a slap to make me realise it was true. **"**

STEVE BRUCE

6

The 1995-96 season saw him an ever-present until injury struck to sideline him in mid-season. Unfortunately Gary Pallister also succumbed to similar problems, and when Bruce returned in 1996 he found Gary Neville his new partner in central defence. Goals seemed few and far between, but he was on the scoresheet against strugglers Bolton in February as if to remind the doubters that he could still hit the back of the net when required.

The long term may see the two Garys, Neville and Pallister, at the heart of the United back four, leaving Steve Bruce to pursue future dreams elsewhere. If and when he takes that step, it will be with the thanks of everyone from the directors down, because though England may have overlooked him, Steve Bruce's part in past glories is a major one.

MANCHESTER UNITED FC HISTORY

More than any other team, the name of Manchester United is known and respected anywhere in the world. Players like George Best, Denis Law (the man Bergkamp was named after) and World Cup winner Bobby Charlton have had much to do with that, as have recent heroes like Ryan Giggs and Eric Cantona.

But it was the tragedy of the Munich air disaster on 6 February 1958 that wrote the club's name on the front pages as well as the back. Eight players lost their lives, and names like Duncan Edwards, Roger Byrne, Bill Whelan and Tommy Taylor have since gone down in football folklore.

Manchester United's worldwide reputation began in 1878 as Newton Heath. By finishing behind Nottingham Forest in the Football Alliance in 1892, the Heathens were promoted straight into an enlarged Division One. And that's where they've stayed for the majority of the time since.

After relegation in their second season, Newton Heath shut up shop in 1902. A new club, Manchester United, was immediately formed and within six years stars such as Billy Meredith and Alex 'Sandy' Turnbull were toasting the Red Devils' first League Championship.

An FA Cup triumph preceded another title win in 1910-11, United's first season at their new Old Trafford stadium after moving from Clayton. It was

Honours Board

1896-97	Division Two Runners-up	1966-67	Division One Champions
1905-06	Division Two Runners-up	1967-68	Division One Runners-up, European Cup Winners and World Club Championship Runners-up
1907-08	Division One Champions		
1908-09	FA Cup Winners	1974-75	Division Two Champions
1910-11	Division One Champions	1975-76	FA Cup Runners-up
1924-25	Division Two Runners-up	1976-77	FA Cup Winners
1935-36	Division Two Champions	1978-79	FA Cup Runners-up
1937-38	Division Two Runners-up	1979-80	Division One Runners-up
1946-47	Division One Runners-up	1982-83	FA Cup Winners and League Cup Runners-up
1947-48	Division One Runners-up and FA Cup Winners	1984-85	FA Cup Winners
1948-49	Division One Runners-up	1987-88	Division One Runners-up
1950-51	Division One Runners-up	1989-90	FA Cup Winners
1951-52	Division One Champions	1990-91	League Cup Runners-up, European Cup Winners' Cup Winners and Super Cup Winners
1955-56	Division One Champions		
1956-57	Division One Champions and FA Cup Runners-up	1991-92	Division One Runners-up and League Cup Winners
1957-58	FA Cup Runners-up	1992-93	Premier League Champions
1958-59	Division One Runners-up	1993-94	Premier League Champions, FA Cup Winners and League Cup Runners-up
1962-63	FA Cup Winners		
1963-64	Division One Runners-up	1994-95	Premier League Runners-up and FA Cup Runners-up
1964-65	Division One Champions	1995-96	Premier League Champions and FA Cup Finalists

MANCHESTER UNITED FC *Factfile*

Year formed:	1878
Ground:	Old Trafford, Manchester M16 0RA
Nickname:	The Red Devils
Club colours:	Red, white and black
Manager:	Alex Ferguson
Record attendance:	70,504 v Aston Villa, 27 December 1920, Division One
Record League victory:	10-1 v Wolverhampton Wanderers, 15 October 1892, Division One
	- Scorers: Stewart 3, Donaldson 3, Farman, Hood, Carson, Hendry
Record Cup victory:	10-0 v RSC Anderlecht, 26 September 1956, European Cup Preliminary Round second leg
	- Scorers: Viollet 4, Taylor 3, Whelan 2, Berry
Record defeat:	0-7 v Blackburn Rovers, 10 April 1926, Division One;
	0-7 v Aston Villa, 27 December 1930, Division One;
	0-7 v Wolverhampton Wanderers, 26 December 1931, Division Two
Highest League scorer in a season:	Dennis Viollet, 32, 1959-60, Division One
Highest League scorer during career:	Bobby Charlton, 199, 1956-73
Most League appearances:	Bobby Charlton, 606, 1956-73

to be another 37 years, however, before success returned to the red half of Manchester.

United took three League titles in the 1950s and the scene was set for Matt Busby's 'Babes' to become England's ambassadors in Europe – but the Munich tragedy smashed their dreams.

Busby was forced to rebuild, and he did so in grand style: ten years later Manchester United became the first English club to win the European Cup. The team, including Charlton, Best and Crerand, beat Benfica 4-1 at Wembley.

Busby's retirement in January 1969 signalled a decline in the club's fortunes. Current manager, Alex Ferguson, was the man who ended the long Championship exile in 1992-93 as Hughes, Robson and Bruce helped the club clinch the Premiership title in that competition's first two seasons. The second win was coupled with an FA Cup victory over Chelsea, making United only the third team this century to achieve the coveted Double.

1994-95 saw United pipped at the post in both major competitions, finishing Premiership runners-up behind Blackburn and beaten finalists in the FA Cup – but with the title wait over, the next milestone fans were looking forward to was a second European Cup victory.

With the exception of record signing Andy Cole, it seemed the new wave of Red Devils would be home-grown articles, the Neville brothers, Butt, Beckham and Scholes just five of the promising lads to make a first-team mark in the mid 1990s. From Busby Babes to Fergie's Faves? Only time will tell.

CANTONA

He may be the man everybody loves to hate – but Eric Cantona is without doubt one of the most talented individuals in the Premiership. It's a bonus that he appears to have controlled his fiery temperament, after missing the tail-end of the 1994-95 season and the first seven games of the following campaign, following an assault on a foul-mouthed fan.

But the fabulous Frenchman returned with a vengeance, scoring a penalty in the 2-2 draw with Liverpool at Old Trafford at the beginning of October – and his form remained sky-high in the months that followed, as United pursued Newcastle in an attempt to clinch what would be their third Premiership title in four years. Little wonder Alex Ferguson had a smile on his face!

England has proved a good hunting ground for Cantona. Despite being overlooked by Trevor Francis' Sheffield Wednesday, he arrived at Elland Road in February 1992 and played 15 times as Leeds went on to clinch the title. Ironically, the team they pipped to the post was...Manchester United!

But by the end of the year, he'd become an Old Trafford regular in a £1.2 million deal which has since proved one of the bargains of the decade. And Leeds had to pay £3.4 million to replace him with Tony Yeboah.

Cantona's ability to play his team-mates into dangerous positions, coupled with his own goalscoring prowess, inspired the Red Devils to top the Premiership in its first two campaigns, bringing the Championship to Old Trafford for the first time since Sir Matt Busby's reign. United's FA Cup win in 1994, humbling Chelsea 4-0 thanks to a brace of ice-cool Cantona penalties, added even

> "Eric has a vast amount of flair and quality and an eye for goal. If you give an international player like him a lot of space he's going to show his quality. He does things off the cuff and when they come off he looks really good. If they don't he doesn't let it worry him too much."

DAVID BURROWS

ERIC CANTONA *Factfile*

Birthdate:	24 May 1966
Birthplace:	Marseilles, France
Height:	6' 1"
Weight:	13st 7lb

League Record (To start of 1995-96 season)

FROM-TO	CLUB	APPS	GOALS
1983-88	Auxerre	81	23
1988-89	Marseilles	22	5
1988-89	Bordeaux	11	6
1989-90	Montpellier	33	10
1990-91	Marseilles	18	8
1991-92	Nimes	17	2
1991-92	Leeds United	28	9
1992-95	Manchester United	77	39
Total		287	102

more lustre to Ferguson's record as United's most successful manager during the last quarter of a century.

It's arguable that, had Cantona not missed the run-in to the 1994-95 title, United might have registered a hat-trick of wins (a feat achieved just three times in history) and successfully defended their Double. As it was, Jack Walker's Blackburn won the trophy after a nailbiting last day of the season and Everton emerged victorious at Wembley, with Paul Rideout scoring the game's only goal.

Cantona had arrived from the continent leaving a cloud of controversy behind him, thanks to reports of misconduct against both fellow players and officials. His career record, which listed six French clubs in just eight years – though this does not include two separate spells with Auxerre and Marseilles – suggested he was one of soccer's journeymen, but he seems to have found his spiritual home at Old Trafford. Alex Ferguson persevered with a player former managers had found too difficult to handle and has been rewarded with many outstanding performances. All seemed to be coming right for Cantona, and his Player of the Year award was well deserved.

SCHMEICHEL

PETER SCHMEICHEL *Factfile*

Born:	18 November 1963
Birthplace:	Gladsaxe, Denmark
Height:	6' 4"
Weight:	14st 0lb

League Record (To start of 1995-96 season)

FROM-TO	CLUB	APPS	GOALS
1991-95	Manchester United	154	—

If Bruce Grobbelaar was the first 'sweeper keeper', then Peter Schmeichel can claim to be the first centre-forward who can use his hands! So often when the game has hung on a single goal, the mighty Dane has lumbered forward into the opposing penalty area to add his considerable height and weight to the attack, as he did successfully against Rotor Volgograd in the UEFA Cup. Bookies have even started quoting odds on him scoring in a game, currently 50-1 – and you get the feeling his number might just come up soon!

Well known for bawling out his defence when he considers they've let him down, the Great Dane bosses his area like no other Number 1 today, adding enormously to the confidence of the Neville brothers as they've come through to become first-team regulars. It's easier to take chances and impress when you've a reliable last line of defence behind you...and the occasional ear-bashing is a small price to pay. Attackers too are delighted with his long, accurate throws which set up many a breakaway for speedy flankers like Giggs and Sharpe.

United's acceleration in the title chase, that saw Newcastle's 12-point lead dwindle to nothing, was based on two factors – the goals of Eric Cantona and the shot-stopping of Schmeichel at the other end. After starting the new year of 1996 disastrously with a 4-1 reverse at White Hart Lane, the next ten games saw just three goals conceded.

There's no doubt that in the five years since joining the club from Brondby for £550,000, Peter the Great has written his name large in Old Trafford folklore alongside such goalkeeping greats as Gregg, Stepney and Bailey. Many thousands of lime-green keepers' jerseys have made their way out of the Old Trafford merchandise concessions, underlining the fact that the man is a great role model. Back home, too, his record of 73 international caps (to the start of the 1995-96 season) is constantly being added to: with country as with club, his is the first name that makes it to the team sheet.

Loud, outspoken but supremely talented, Peter Schmeichel has a medals haul to match: with three Danish Championships and a European Championship with Denmark in 1992 to add to his achievements since arriving at Old Trafford. Twenty-one clean sheets in 1994-95 gives him a record to aim at, but there's little doubt he'd settle for sharing glory with the team.

❝It's made a lot easier for me that I play behind such a great defence. Gary Pallister and Steve Bruce give me great protection. A dustbin could have kept goal for us in some games, the defence has been that good. ❞

PETER SCHMEICHEL

PALLISTER

Gary Pallister's signing in August 1989 made him the club's record buy at £2.3 million, the move taking place during Michael Knighton's short spell in charge. Unlike the short-lived would-be chairman, he was very much still part of the Old Trafford scene in 1996, though his 1995-96 season was spoiled by a back injury which threatened to keep him out of the summer's European Championships.

He'd fought back from disappointment before: a local businessman had paid his first few months' wages when cash-strapped Middlesbrough signed him and, as with United's two million-plus investment, he proved value for money. His pay packet has gone up a bit since then, though: he started at a not so princely £60 a week!

Having arrived at Old Trafford, he immediately forged an impressive partnership with Steve Bruce and gathered an amazing amount of silverware in his first five seasons. International recognition came in 1987-88 against Hungary after nine B appearances, and he became a regular once at Old Trafford. A record of one game missed in two seasons (1993-95) shows what an England regular he became.

Old Trafford fans know how important Gary is to club as well as country, but his 1995-96 season ground to a painful halt after an ever-present first three months. Gary Neville is an outstanding prospect, but Pallister's dominating presence was – and is – invaluable.

Did You Know?

Gary is held in highest regard by his fellow professionals and was PFA Player of the Year in 1992.

GARY PALLISTER *Factfile*

Born:	30 June 1965
Birthplace:	Ramsgate
Height:	6' 4"
Weight:	13st 0lb

League Record (To start of 1995-96 season)

FROM-TO	CLUB	APPS	GOALS
1985-86	Darlington (loan)	7	–
1985-90	Middlesbrough	156	5
1989-95	Manchester Utd	236	8
Total		399	13

BUTT

Nicky Butt's inclusion in the starting line-up in Manchester United's first 15 League games of last season, 1995-96, may have surprised some people – but to the Manchester United faithful, his inclusion in the midfield was recognition that this young man, just 20 when the campaign started, had indeed come of age.

With just two dozen League games (and three England Under 21 caps) to his credit before the season kicked off, he showed by his poise, assurance and aggression that the absence of former midfield dynamo Paul Ince, surprisingly sold to Inter Milan in the summer, would not make the difference that had been assumed. Now we realised why Alex Ferguson had cashed in on 'the Guv'nor'...perhaps we were watching the 'new Guv'nor'!

He didn't often weigh in with goals – that wasn't his job – but when he did they were important. One against Sunderland in the FA Cup Third Round helped bring about a replay, while a strike at Old Trafford against Liverpool secured another draw. He obviously enjoyed the feeling, for struggling Bolton also tasted the Butt boot as the ball nestled in the net.

It's tough for any home-town boy to claim a place in the team given the high-priced competition he faces. Yet the evidence is that Alex Ferguson knows quality when he sees it – so, by now, do we! And there's no ifs and Butts...

NICKY BUTT *Factfile*

Born:	21 January 1975
Birthplace:	Manchester
Height:	5' 10"
Weight:	11st 1lb

League Record (To start of 1995-96 season)

FROM-TO	CLUB	APPS	GOALS
1993-95	Manchester United	24	1

MANCHESTER UTD
Story Of A Season, 1995-96

Three Premierships in four years? A tall order, to be sure – but the Red Devils were undoubtedly the team to show the dream could be made reality.

AUGUST

Three wins and an opening-day defeat as the season got under way... yet without a certain Frenchman! Beating Blackburn was sweet revenge for last year.

19	Aston Villa	(A)	1-3	Beckham
23	West Ham Utd	(H)	2-1	Scholes, Keane
26	Wimbledon	(H)	3-1	Keane 2, Cole
28	Blackburn R	(A)	2-1	Sharpe, Beckham

P	W	D	L	F-A	Position
4	3	—	1	8-6	4

SEPTEMBER

Despite two games away from Old Trafford, an unbeaten month saw the Red Devils shift up a gear – and a place in the table – with three forwards on the mark

9	Everton	(A)	3-2	Sharpe 2, Giggs
16	Bolton W	(H)	3-0	Scholes 2, Giggs
23	Sheffield Wed	(A)	0-0	

P	W	D	L	F-A	Position
3	2	1	—	6-2	3

OCTOBER

It's shaping up for a two-horse race, as United move within striking distance of Newcastle United. Again, an unbeaten month – and that man's back with a goal!

1	Liverpool	(H)	2-2	Butt, Cantona (*pen*)
14	Manchester C	(H)	1-0	Scholes
21	Chelsea	(A)	4-1	Scholes 2, Giggs, McClair
28	Middlesbrough	(H)	2-0	Pallister, Cole

P	W	D	L	F-A	Position
4	3	1	—	9-3	2

NOVEMBER

A rare slip-up at Highbury, but no slip down the table as two thrashings of relegation strugglers spreads the goals around – and Choccy gets sent to Coventry!

4	Arsenal	(A)	0-1	
18	Southampton	(H)	4-1	Giggs 2, Scholes, Cole
22	Coventry C	(A)	4-0	Irwin, McClair 2, Beckham
27	Nott'm Forest	(A)	1-1	Cantona (*pen*)

P	W	D	L	F-A	Position
4	2	1	1	9-3	2

DECEMBER

Two wins, two draws and two losses as United show they're human after all. But there's little doubt, as they retain second place, that they're still ahead of the pack.

2	Chelsea	(H)	1-1	Beckham
9	Sheffield Wed	(H)	2-2	Cantona 2
17	Liverpool	(A)	0-2	
24	Leeds Utd	(A)	1-3	Cole
27	Newcastle Utd	(H)	2-0	Cole, Keane
30	QPR	(H)	2-1	Cole, Giggs

P	W	D	L	F-A	Position
6	2	2	2	8-9	2

oca-Cola Cup

| York C | (H) | 0-3 | |
| York C | (A) | 3-1 | Scholes 2, Cooke |

UEFA Cup

R1	Rotor Volgograd	(A)	0-0	
R1	Rotor Volgograd	(H)	2-2	Scholes, Schmeichel
	Rotor Volgograd win on away goals			

JANUARY

With Cup matters on their mind, this is another mixed month for United by Fergie's high standards. Now down to third, were the cracks emerging?

1	Tottenham H	(A)	1-4	Cole
13	Aston Villa	(H)	0-0	
22	West Ham Utd	(A)	1-0	Cantona

P	W	D	L	F-A	Position
3	1	1	1	2-4	3

FEBRUARY

All questions are answered with a 100 per cent month. Thirteen goals were unlucky for four opponents, and sent a warning to Tyneside.

3	Wimbledon	(A)	4-2	Cole, Perry (og), Cantona 2
10	Blackburn R	(H)	1-0	Sharpe
21	Everton	(H)	2-0	Keane, Giggs
25	Bolton W	(A)	6-0	Beckham, Bruce, Cole, Scholes 2, Butt

P	W	D	L	F-A	Position
4	4	—	—	13-2	2

MARCH

Eric's month, as four goals bring ten points – the draw at Loftus Road being achieved against all the odds. Footballer of the Year? No question!

4	Newcastle Utd	(A)	1-0	Cantona
16	QPR	(A)	1-1	Cantona
20	Arsenal	(H)	1-0	Cantona
24	Tottenham H	(H)	1-0	Cantona

P	W	D	L	F-A	Position
4	3	1	—	4-1	1

APRIL

It's nip and tuck now at the top as United pile on the pressure. A poor show at the Dell – those grey shirts are blamed – but normal service soon resumes.

6	Manchester C	(A)	3-2	Cantona (pen), Cole, Giggs
8	Coventry C	(H)	1-0	Cantona
13	Southampton	(A)	1-3	Giggs
17	Leeds Utd	(H)	1-0	Keane
27	Nott'm Forest	(H)	5-0	Scholes, Beckham 2, Giggs, Cantona

P	W	D	L	F-A	Position
5	4	—	1	11-5	1

MAY

A nailbiting season ends, and Fergie's quest for a second historic Double reaches its climax – the first leg a reunion with Bryan Robson.

| 5 | Middlesbrough | (A) | 3-0 | May, Cole, Giggs |

P	W	D	L	F-A	Position
1	1	—	—	3-0	1

Littlewoods FA Cup

R3	Sunderland	(H)	2-2	Butt, Cantona
R3r	Sunderland	(A)	2-1	Scholes, Cole
R4	Reading	(A)	3-0	Giggs, Parker, Cantona
R5	Manchester C	(H)	2-1	Cantona (pen), Sharpe
R6	Southampton	(H)	2-0	Cantona, Sharpe
SF	Chelsea		2-1	Cole, Beckham
F	Liverpool		1-0	Cantona

IRWIN

In a team as star-studded as United's, it's impossible for every player to catch the eye. Irishman Denis Irwin is undoubtedly one of the less noticeable of Alex Ferguson's first eleven – and since Eric Cantona started taking penalties, he's become even less conspicuous. Yet no one at Old Trafford would minimise the contribution the quietly confident full-back has made since arriving from nearby Oldham Athletic in 1990.

The 1995-96 season saw him pass the 200 League game landmark in red and white, but he was a vastly experienced performer long before a £625,000 fee persuaded manager Joe Royle to let him leave Boundary Park. The clincher that won him the move was his cool, classy display against United in that year's FA Cup semi-final. 'He'd been on our shortlist before,' revealed Alex Ferguson, 'but that underlined his potential.'

He'd learned his trade at Elland Road, Leeds, where he's been an apprentice, and made 72 appearances in the all white at League level before being released in 1986. Yet Oldham was where he really shone, being recognised by his fellow professionals in 1990 who voted him into the Second Division PFA team.

His ability to play on either side of the defence (as well as delivering pinpoint inswinging corners) would prove highly useful, as Alex Ferguson turned United into the most successful team of the 1990s. Their success led to a higher international profile for Denis, who played his first Eire game two matches into his United career. Since that debut against Morocco, he's become a regular choice for country as well as club.

DENIS IRWIN *Factfile*

Born:	31 October 1965
Birthplace:	Cork
Height:	5' 8"
Weight:	11st 0lb

League Record (To start of 1995-96 season)

FROM-TO	CLUB	APPS	GOALS
1983-86	Leeds United	72	1
1986-90	Oldham Athletic	167	4
1990-95	Manchester United	194	13
Total		433	18

DID YOU KNOW?

Denis' outstanding form towards the end of last season kept current England international Gary Neville out of the side.

NEVILLE

Gary Neville's rise to fame and fortune has been amazing by any standards. Son of Bury FC's secretary (his mum also works for the club), he understandably chose Old Trafford over Gigg Lane...yet his was a name known only to a select few until making his club debut as substitute in a 1992 UEFA Cup tie against Moscow Torpedo. His appearance then lasted just two minutes, while he played only a single game in the second Championship season, against Coventry in May 1994.

As the 1994-95 campaign started, Gary Neville remained on the fringes of the United squad...yet stands in 1996 as first-choice right-back for club and country. Two years older than brother Philip, he prefers to play as a central defender, but at right-back can use his long throw to add to his team's attacking armoury.

Injuries to Pallister and Bruce saw him at centre-back for much of 1995-96, but he took his full international bow at Wembley against Japan in the 1995 Umbro Cup at full-back. He's since kept Newcastle's Warren Barton and Liverpool's Rob Jones out of the side, and was first choice coming into the European Championships.

Though not the tallest of defenders, Gary's intelligent distribution and shrewd positional sense seem developed beyond his still tender years, and more than make up for physical slightness. In terms of long-term potential, Old Trafford has few brighter...

GARY NEVILLE *Factfile*

Born:	18 February 1975
Birthplace:	Bury
Height:	5' 10"
Weight:	11st 7lb

League Record (To start of 1995-96 season)

FROM-TO	CLUB	APPS	GOALS
1994-95	Manchester United	19	—

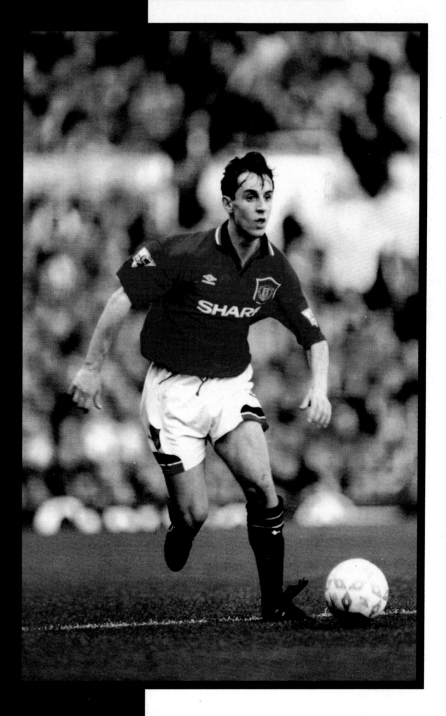

Several rainforests have already been felled in extolling the virtues of Ryan Giggs, the teenage winger who is undeniably the single biggest star to emerge from Manchester United's youth policy since the 1960s. Reebok, his boot sponsors, have even made a TV ad in which George Best, no less, sings his praises along with a host of other sporting and showbiz celebrities. Little wonder Alex Ferguson originally shielded the teenage prodigy (the PFA Young Player of the Year for 1992 and 1993) from the media in case his natural talents went the way of Best's.

Yet despite the occasional blip in form, notably in the early part of the 1994-95 season when a niggling calf injury took its toll on his speed, Giggs has remained happily level-headed. He's a regular choice for Wales, his country of birth, which he chose to represent after having represented England at schoolboy level.

Having missed the early stages of 1995-96, Giggs returned to action in a difficult away game in the UEFA Cup against Rotor Volgograd and could have had a hat-trick without the reflexes of keeper Andrei Samorukov. 'He should be very pleased with himself,' said Alex Ferguson. 'He did a very useful job.' Useful isn't a word usually associated with Ryan Giggs – spectacular, of course, is. And after three subs' appearances in the League, scoring the winner in a 3-2 thriller against Everton, he reclaimed his place and would thereafter regularly be found on the scoresheet.

A brace against Southampton saw the strugglers clinically dispatched in front of an Old Trafford crowd. His career strike rate of one goal in five games is likely to be upped considerably by such performances. Nor were his goals often 'normal'

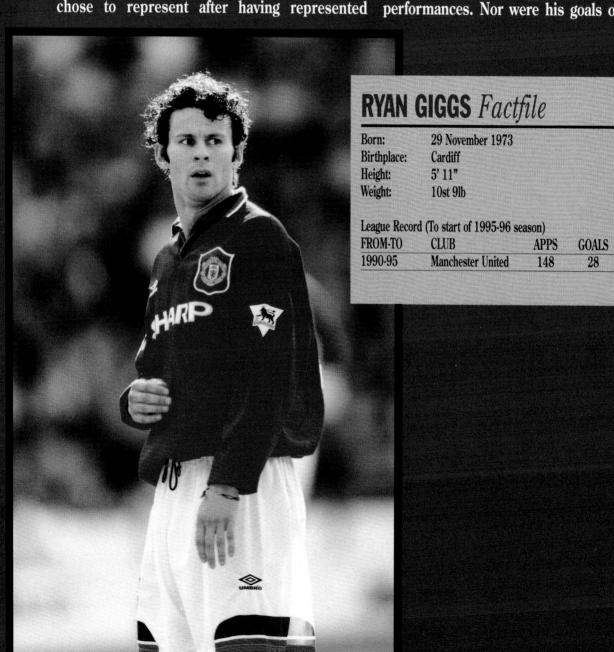

RYAN GIGGS *Factfile*

Born:	29 November 1973
Birthplace:	Cardiff
Height:	5' 11"
Weight:	10st 9lb

League Record (To start of 1995-96 season)

FROM-TO	CLUB	APPS	GOALS
1990-95	Manchester United	148	28

ones. His winner against Manchester City in the third local derby of the 1995-96 season in April was a masterpiece, angled so finely into the top corner that almost everybody in Maine Road, including his manager, assumed it had hit the side netting.

Still only 22, Ryan passed his 150 League appearances for United during the season (his first was back in 1991 as a substitute against Everton), and it seems inconceivable that Manchester United could ever let him go.

> **"I don't think I'm anything like George Best except for my age and the fact I play for United. Best was a great player and hopefully one day I can be as good as him."**
> **RYAN GIGGS**

Along with Cameroon striker Roger Milla, United midfield man Lee Sharpe's gone into football folklore for an unusual method of celebrating a goal. Both involve the corner flag and Elvis Presley-style gyrations, but that's where the similarities end. Because Lee, unlike the veteran African, has many years left at the top.

His versatility in the left-sided positions has given him several chances to shine in the wide left, central midfield and left-back positions. When in finest attacking form, he's even managed to displace Ryan Giggs from his usual left-wing berth to the right.

He was playing for Torquay United when the call came to go north to Old Trafford in 1988. He'd only signed professional a couple of weeks before, so a £60,000 fee (rising to £200,000 in instalments) was considerable reward for the west country club who'd nurtured his talent. Ironically, Lee, who was born at Halesowen near Birmingham, could have been the second Sharpe at Old Trafford: younger brother John was a triallist for United before being offered an apprenticeship at Maine Road.

Lee's Old Trafford career really took off when he hit a League Cup hat-trick against Arsenal at Highbury in November 1990. The 6-2 win made football sit up, take notice and ask questions – and newly confirmed national boss Graham Taylor was one of those who had an interest in the answer.

England honours came for Lee with a debut against Eire in March the following year – a European Championship qualifier. The PFA Young Player of the Year accolade followed that same month, but his fast-rising career was suddenly put on hold by the double blow of a niggling groin injury and a spell of meningitis. He was out of action for more or less a season, before exploding to life in November of United's first Premiership season. It's been onwards and upwards ever since.

The 1995-96 season saw him ever-present for the first eight League games, before becoming a regular substitute – a victim of his own adaptability. But goals against Blackburn, Everton (2) and the winner against Manchester City that helped United on the road to Wembley, will never be forgotten by the faithful. Still just 25, Lee's sure to have a bright future – after all, any club with Sharpe and Keane in their midfield have a lot going for them!

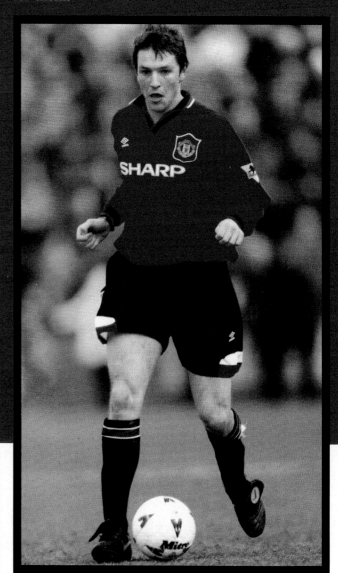

LEE SHARPE *Factfile*

Born:	25 May 1971
Birthplace:	Halesowen
Height:	5' 11"
Weight:	11st 4lb

League Record (To start of 1995-96 season)

FROM-TO	CLUB	APPS	GOALS
1987-88	Torquay United	14	3
1988-95	Manchester United	162	17
Total		176	20

THE SUPERTEAM

HOW MUCH DO *YOU* KNOW ABOUT UNITED?

1 Who was bought from Cambridge and sent to Coventry after two seasons?

2 With which club (apart from United) did Eric Cantona win an English Championship medal?

3 Which player, known as the Guv'nor, left Old Trafford for the San Siro in 1995?

4 Which other club did Alex Ferguson steer to the European Cup Winners' Cup?

5 Which former striker was known as 'Sparky'?

6 Which former United playing favourite is now a club director?

7 How many FA Cup Finals has Peter Schmeichel played in for United?

8 For which country does Denis Irwin play?

9 Which end of the Old Trafford ground used to be the terrace where the home fans stood?

10 In which year did United win the European Cup?

CHALLENGE

11 From which club was Lee Sharpe signed?

12 What is The Cliff?

13 Which colour strip was abandoned in April 1996 as it was not 'visible' enough?

14 Against which team did Peter Schmeichel head his European goal?

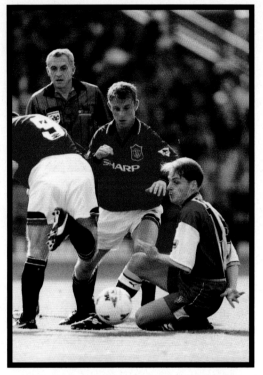

15 Which number did Roy Keane wear during his first seasons at the club?

16 Which team did United play in the 1996 FA Cup Final?

17 Which goalkeeper was sold to Middlesbrough during the course of last season?

18 What is Brian McClair's nickname?

19 Name United's assistant manager who also once played for City.

20 Which player, once United and England captain, now manages another Premiership team?

COLE

DID YOU KNOW?

Despite his scoring problems, Andy Cole kept his first-team place until the end of April 1996 when he was temporarily replaced by Paul Scholes.

Discovered at Highbury, Andy Cole became England's most feared forward when his strike rate and pace shot Newcastle United to the top. Kevin Keegan shocked the football world by paying out a club record £1.75 million in March 1993, and again when he let the hitman move to arch-rivals United for an English record £6 million, plus winger Keith Gillespie, two years later.

Cole settled in quickly, scoring 12 goals in United's final 18 Premiership games to earn a runner's-up medal, and made his England debut in a goalless draw at Wembley with Uruguay. Yet things wouldn't be easy the following year, as the Uniteds of Manchester and Newcastle fought their own league within a league for the Premiership. Andy found himself a marked man, and, with opposing crowds on his back, found his misses as acclaimed as other people's goals.

It was all a far cry from Bristol City, where Cole's acceleration into space and eye for goal had first started ripping defences apart. He'd also spent

some time on loan with Fulham, but made a permanent move west only when it became clear he had no future as a Gunner – one decision George Graham must still regret to this day.

Cole's first full season at Old Trafford in 1995-96 season brought cynics as well as plaudits, but even though he couldn't maintain his stunning scoring rate for Alex Ferguson's team, he certainly put in 100 per cent effort like the professional he is. Another few inches here and there and the goals would come flooding back – yet there was no lack of self-belief.

His all-round game, linking with the brilliance of Cantona and Giggs, improved, but the prolific scoring streak of Paul Scholes put him under further pressure to succeed. It's unlikely the pressure will let up, though his heavily marked presence in the penalty box may well help his fellow forwards find space. At the age of 24, though, the best may yet be to come for Andy Cole and United's fans. Don't discount him for England, either...

ANDY COLE *Factfile*

Born:	15 October 1971
Birthplace:	Nottingham
Height:	5' 10"
Weight:	11st 2lb

League Record (To start of 1995-96 season)

FROM-TO	CLUB	APPS	GOALS
1990-91	Arsenal	1	—
1991-92	Fulham (loan)	13	3
1991-92	Bristol City (loan)	12	8
1992-93	Bristol City	29	12
1992-95	Newcastle United	70	55
1994-95	Manchester United	18	12
Total		143	90

KEANE

Rarely has a player been as aptly named as Roy Keane, the Eire international midfielder whose energetic pursuit of man and ball in midfield has made him an integral part of Manchester United's search for further honours in the 1990s.

Keane's remarkable engine permitted him to make lung-bursting box-to-box runs at will, fitting smoothly into the space vacated by the legendary Bryan Robson when he departed to Middlesbrough in 1994.

The Roy Keane story had started when Brian Clough brought him to English football from Irish side Cobh Ramblers. The £10,000 he paid in 1990 soon looked like the bargain of the decade, as Roy the boy grew up very quickly indeed. He had to – he made his debut against Liverpool, discovering there were no easy games in the élite. There were disciplinary problems on the way, his volatile temper leading to confrontation with players and referees in the early days, but he managed to score over 30 goals in around 150 games in all competitions.

The 1994-95 season saw him filling in at right-back in the absence through injury of Paul Parker, and even sometimes in the middle of the back four. The previous year, of course, had seen them take the Double, with Keane very much in the driving seat. And it wasn't surprising to see him repeating the feat in 1995-96 with another Wembley date – another clash with Liverpool.

He'd not enjoyed the best of season through injury and suspension, despite scoring the winner in United's first home game of the campaign against West Ham.

With 28 Eire caps before the start of last season, Keane is still only 25 and, providing he can keep his temper in check, has the skills to become one of the United legends.

Did You Know?

Roy starred for Eire in the 1994 World Cup, and though he returned in need of a hernia operation, put it off to play for his club.

ANSWERS

HOW DID YOU RATE?

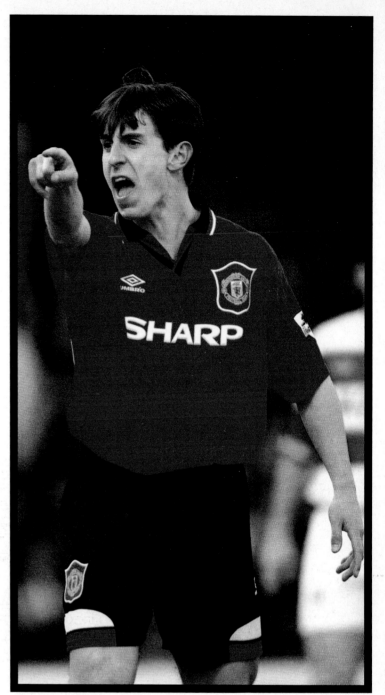

1	Dion Dublin
2	Leeds United
3	Paul Ince
4	Aberdeen
5	Mark Hughes
6	Sir Bobby Charlton
7	Three
8	Eire
9	The Stretford End
10	1968

11	Torquay United
12	United's training ground
13	Grey
14	Rotor Volgograd
15	18
16	Liverpool
17	Gary Walsh
18	Choccy
19	Brian Kidd
20	Bryan Robson